CROWS!

STRANGE AND WONDERFUL

BY LAURENCE PRINGLE
ILLUSTRATED BY BOB MARSTALL

Boyds Mills Press
Honesdale, Pennsylvania

For Bob Marstall, a fine artist and a good
companion in both civilized and wild places.

— L. P.

For Patricia Lee Lewis—poet, writer, teacher,
traveler, and friend—whose Texas-flavored
blend of grace and grit inspires me, and whose
encouragement and advice steadies me.

— B. M.

Acknowledgments

The author wishes to thank Dr. Kevin McGowan, Cornell Vertebrate Collections, Cornell University; and Dr. Donald F. Caccamise, Professor and Head, Department of Fishery and Wildlife Sciences, New Mexico State University, for their valuable assistance.

The artist wishes to thank Barbara Scully of *The Whistling Crow* in Shelburne Falls, Massachusetts, and Mark Kelly of *Wild Encounters* in Hopkinton, Massachusetts,—licensed "crow rehabbers" who helped greatly in his search for flight-challenged crows to use as models. Special thanks to Diane De Groat for permission to photograph her three stuffed crows; to John Zokowski of *Butler-Dearden Paper Service*, and to Barbara De Vitto of *Hunt Photo and Video* of Melrose, Massachusetts, for introducing him to the Hahnemuhle line of "digital fine-art" papers.

Artist's Note

The art for this book was prepared by using my computer and an Epson Stylus Color 1520 inkjet printer to transfer my pencil drawings onto a Hahnemuhle digitally prepared watercolor paper ("Wm. Turner," 190g), which was then coated with two layers of acrylic matte medium and painted with oils in the usual way.

Boyds Mills Press, Inc.
815 Church Street
Honesdale, Pennsylvania 18431
Printed in China

Publisher Cataloging-in-Publication Data

Pringle, Laurence.
   Crows! : strange and wonderful / by Laurence Pringle : illustrated by Bob Marstall. —1st ed.
[32] p. : col. ill. ;   cm.
Summary: An introduction to the life and behavior of crows.
ISBN 978-1-56397-899-9 (hc) • ISBN 978-1-59078-724-3 (pb)
1. Crows—Juvenile literature. (1. Crows.) I. Marstall, Bob. II. Title.
598.964 21   CIP   QL696.P2367 2002
2001092591

First edition
First Boyds Mills Press paperback edition, 2010
The text of this book is set in 15-point Clearface regular.

10 9 8 7 6 5 4 3   (hc)
10 9 8 7 6 5 4 3 2 1 (pb)

Caw . . . Caw . . . Caw!

A crow's voice is bold and sassy. Almost everyone has heard it.

We know crows by their calls. We know them by their large size—they are about twenty inches long—and by their glossy black feathers. Crows are not plain black, though. If you get close to a crow, you may see glints of deep blue and purple on its feathers.

Crows are often seen and heard, but to most people they are birds of mystery.

5

DROP
LITTER
HERE

It is not easy to get close to crows. They are smart. They know that humans are sometimes their enemies. They manage to find safe places to raise their young, and they find food where millions of people live. You can often see crows hunting for food alongside roads, in parking lots and city parks, and on suburban lawns.

The crow you have most likely seen is the American or common crow. It lives in parts of every state, except Hawaii, and far north in Canada. The common crow has relatives all over the world. Its bird family, the *Corvidae*, includes rooks, jackdaws, magpies, and jays.

American Crow

Blue Jay

Rook

Jackdaw

Magpie

8

A smaller crow, the fish crow, lives in states along the Atlantic Coast and the Gulf of Mexico. Instead of "caw, caw," it calls out "car, car."

The largest member of the crow family is the common raven—a great dark bird of the Far North and of rugged mountaintops. Its call is a low, hoarse "quork, quork."

American Crow

Fish Crow

Raven

There is nothing "common" about the common raven and the common crow. The raven may be the smartest of all birds, as intelligent as a monkey. Other members of the crow family also have highly developed brains.

Crows show their intelligence in many ways. They are playful. Young crows may play tug-of-war with a twig. They swing upside down on tree branches. Sometimes a crow flies into the air with a stick in its beak, then drops it and swoops down to catch the stick before it hits the ground.

Crows tease other animals. Sometimes a crow gives a playful nip to the tail of a dog or other animal, then flies out of reach. Crows also mimic the calls of other birds. They imitate all sorts of other sounds— a squeaky door, a puppy's yelp, a cat's meow. Tame crows can be taught to say such words as "hello," "good-bye," and "hot dog."

Crows have a complex language. They make at least twenty-five different sounds. Besides cawing in many ways, they growl, squawk, squeal, coo, and rattle. By calling in different ways, a crow can identify itself to other crows, keep in touch with them, and say things to them.

A crow calling "Ko-ko, ko-ko, ko-ko" warns other crows to stay out of its territory. Calling "Caw, caw, caw" in a certain way warns other crows of danger—"Stay away!" Calling "Caw, caw, caw" in a different way has another meaning. For example, a series of quick, hoarse, drawn-out caws is the "assembly" call that urges other crows to come quickly.

At mating time in the spring, a male crow makes cooing and rattling sounds to its mate. They swoop and soar together in the sky. Soon the pair begins to build a nest for the female's eggs. It is usually high in a tall tree, where it is well hidden.

A crow's nest is made of big and little twigs, strips of bark from grapevines, grasses, and rootlets. While building the nest, the older mated crows are helped by young crows that were born a year or two earlier. They are all part of a close and cooperative crow family that may number a dozen birds. The father and the young helpers bring food for the mother crow while she warms the eggs. After the eggs hatch, the father and helpers bring food for the baby crows. The older brothers and sisters also help guard the nest.

Crows are born with blue eyes that gradually turn black as the birds become adults.

Crows are always alert for animals that might be dangerous.
They make scolding calls when a cat walks on the forest floor
beneath their nest. But crows are most concerned about raccoons,
foxes, large hawks, and large owls.

After dark, great-horned owls swoop through forests on silent
wings, sometimes killing sleeping crows for food. When a crow
spies a great-horned owl in the daytime, it gives the "assembly" call.
Every crow within hearing distance hurries in, and a wild crow
rumpus called "mobbing" begins.

Cawing excitedly, dozens of crows perch or fly near the owl.
Some crows may dart in to peck at its back. If the owl moves on its
branch, the crow clamor grows louder. If the owl flies, trying to
reach a safer hiding place, the crows become a roaring black cloud
in pursuit.

Crows themselves are often mobbed by smaller birds, especially during summer nesting time. Blackbirds, king birds, and others sometimes chase crows because crows hunt for their nests and eat eggs and nestlings.

Throughout the seasons, a crow eats any kind of food it can find. In the spring it may walk—crows do not hop as most birds do—through a farmer's field. It grabs insects and worms, and sometimes plucks out newly sprouted corn seedlings. In the summer, it may probe its beak beneath leaves on the ground for earthworms. In the winter, it may search for waste grain left in fields after harvest.

Crows eat mice, snakes, insects, fruit, and animals killed by cars. They eat food people have thrown away, using their strong beaks to rip open plastic garbage bags. In one day, a crow's diet might include berries, pizza, snails, grasshoppers, and some tasty morsels from a dead opossum.

23

Crows get food in clever ways. To eat shellfish such as clams and mussels, crows carry them aloft and then drop them onto rocks or other hard surfaces. The shells crack open, and the crows eat the delicious flesh inside.

Small crows that live on the New Caledonia Islands, east of Australia, make tools of twigs. The crow breaks a twig off a tree in a way that leaves a hook on the twig's end. The crow then inserts the hooked end into a hole in a tree and snags insects with it. These New Caledonia crows store their tools in safe places and use them again and again.

On one occasion, some common crows watched fishermen pull fish up through holes cut in the ice. When some fishing lines were left unattended, the crows pulled the lines out of the water and ate the bait or fish they found on the fishhooks.

As winter approaches, crows may fly just a few hundred miles south or not migrate at all. Each winter night thousands of crows gather to sleep in a grove of trees. By day the crows may fly as far as twenty miles in search of food. At day's end, streams of crows can be seen hurrying home to their special winter roosting place.

People living near a crow roost complain about their noisy neighbors and the birds' droppings. Crows can be pests in other ways, too. Even one crow can damage a vegetable garden, and a large flock of crows can harm wheat, corn, and other farm crops.

Over the span of a year, however, crows eat many insects that harm crops, including wire worms, grasshoppers, cutworms, and weevils. Crows pluck beetle grubs (larvae) from the soil of lawns. Sometimes crows perch on cornstalks and peck at the tops of ripening ears of corn. They eat some corn, but they also eat corn earworms—insect larvae that have harmed the corn.

Crows can do harm, and they can do good. They are simply part of nature. They are fascinating creatures and are among the smartest and most adaptable birds on Earth.

Caw . . . Caw . . . Caw!

Author's Note

Writers are often asked about their first published work. Mine was about crows, and I still feel a twinge of embarrassment when I think of it. Crows fascinated me as I grew up in Hopper Hills, south of Rochester, New York. As I roamed a landscape of farmland and forest, I saw plenty of crows and wondered about their calls and their lives. However, my understanding of crows was mostly based on comments and stories told by farmers and hunters.

One day I witnessed an extraordinary gathering of about thirty crows, cawing excitedly from trees at the edge of a forest. They fled as I crept close but continued their loud chorus in another grove of trees. On the ground I found a freshly killed crow, its stomach torn open.

This seemed to be an example of crow behavior I had heard about from farmers and hunters. I wrote about it and sent my 159-word manuscript to the "True Experiences and Camping Hints" page of *Open Road,* a boys' magazine. My "true experience" was published in the July 1952 issue, and I received a check for $5.00—a lot of money for a sixteen-year-old in those times.

My first published work began, "I've often heard of crows holding trials and executing diseased or disabled crows, but last summer I actually saw it happen." And after describing what I saw, including the dead crow, I concluded, "The crows had apparently decided he was guilty of something and had given him the death sentence."

A few years later, while studying wildlife biology at Cornell University, I learned that I had actually witnessed crow mobbing behavior, which is described on page 20 in this book. The crow I found on the ground had been killed by a predator, probably a hawk or an owl. Other crows gathered and mobbed the predator. There was no trial, and no execution, just a community of crows united against an enemy.

Since then I've learned more about crows from scientists who know them well. They include Dr. Kevin McGowan of Cornell University; Dr. Donald F. Caccamise of New Mexico State University, who corrected errors in the manuscript of this book; and Dr. Nicholas Thompson of Clark University, whose research on crow language inspired my 1976 book, *Listen to the Crows.*

Now I feel lucky to live close to crows year round. In the winter, they roost by the thousands just a few miles away. In the spring, a crow family usually nests in one of the tall spruce trees a few hundred feet from my desk. And in any season, a crow sometimes discovers a great-horned owl resting in a spruce. It gives the assembly call, and then the wild crow rumpus begins, right outside the window of the room in which I wrote these words.